Cross Stitch

Birds of a Feather

Stitch these delightful feathered friends!

2

8

12

18

LEISURE ARTS, INC. • Maumelle, Arkansas

Garden Path

Designed by Barbara Sestok

Nothing is more relaxing than strolling through a garden in full bloom! You can almost smell the flowers and hear the songbirds in this detailed design.

Note: Please read all instructions on page 24 before beginning.

Stitch Count = 110w × 166h

FABRIC SIZE

- One 16" × 20" (40.6cm × 50.8cm) piece of 28-ct. Bluebell Hand-Dyed Jobelan® by Wichelt Imports (stitched over two threads)

DESIGN SIZE

- 28-ct. = 7⁷/₈" × 11⁷/₈" (20.0cm × 30.2cm)

GENERAL INSTRUCTIONS

Center the design and begin stitching over two fabric threads. Work cross stitches and lazy daisy stitches with two strands of cotton embroidery floss. Work French knots, backstitches, and straight stitches with one strand of cotton embroidery floss. Use a pressing cloth to carefully iron the needlework from the back before framing as desired.

GARDEN PATH CHART DIAGRAM

A	B
C	D

CROSS STITCH

ANCHOR		DMC	COLOR
073	K	151	Pale Dusty Rose
118	D	156	Medium Light Blue Violet
234	+	168	Very Light Pewter
235	$	169	Light Pewter
118	V	340	Medium Blue Violet
013	A	349	Dark Coral
010	C	351	Coral
009	J	352	Light Coral
006	B	353	Peach
217	U	367	Dark Pistachio Green
235	G	414	Dark Steel Gray
374	2	420	Dark Hazelnut Brown
1045	&	436	Tan
253	9	472	Ultra Light Avocado Green
683	H	500	Very Dark Blue Green
877	W	502	Blue Green
1042	F	504	Light Blue Green
936	r	632	Ultra Very Dark Desert Sand
256	=	704	Bright Chartreuse
295	>	726	Light Topaz
293	6	727	Very Light Topaz
303	M	742	Light Tangerine
234	E	762	Very Light Pearl Gray
149	N	803	Ultra Very Dark Baby Blue
1011	d	948	Very Light Peach
075	L	962	Medium Dusty Rose

CROSS STITCH

ANCHOR		DMC	COLOR
242	T	989	Forest Green
905	/	3021	Very Dark Brown Gray
267	Z	3346	Hunter Green
266	Y	3347	Medium Yellow Green
263	5	3362	Dark Pine Green
382	#	3371	Black Brown
1030	R	3746	Dark Blue Violet
120	S	3747	Very Light Blue Violet
393	<	3790	Ultra Dark Beige Gray
278	3	3819	Light Moss Green
306	4	3820	Dark Straw
028	P	3832	Medium Raspberry
177	Q	3838	Dark Lavender Blue
1003	n	3853	Dark Autumn Gold
313	8	3854	Medium Autumn Gold
376	t	3864	Light Mocha Beige
001	O	B5200	Snow White

FRENCH KNOT

ANCHOR		DMC	COLOR
009	•	352	Light Coral
295	•	726	Light Topaz
075	•	962	Medium Dusty Rose
382	•	3371	Black Brown
1030	•	3746	Dark Blue Violet
028	•	3832	Medium Raspberry

BACKSTITCH

ANCHOR	DMC	COLOR
1045	436	Tan
683	500	Very Dark Blue Green
905	3021	Very Dark Brown Gray
382	3371	Black Brown
278	3819	Light Moss Green
177	3838	Dark Lavender Blue
376	3864	Light Mocha Beige

STRAIGHT STITCH

ANCHOR	DMC	COLOR
118	340	Medium Blue Violet
217	367	Dark Pistachio Green
256	704	Bright Chartreuse
303	742	Light Tangerine

LAZY DAISY

ANCHOR	DMC	COLOR
118	340	Medium Blue Violet

Gray area indicates last row of previous section of design.

Garden Path A

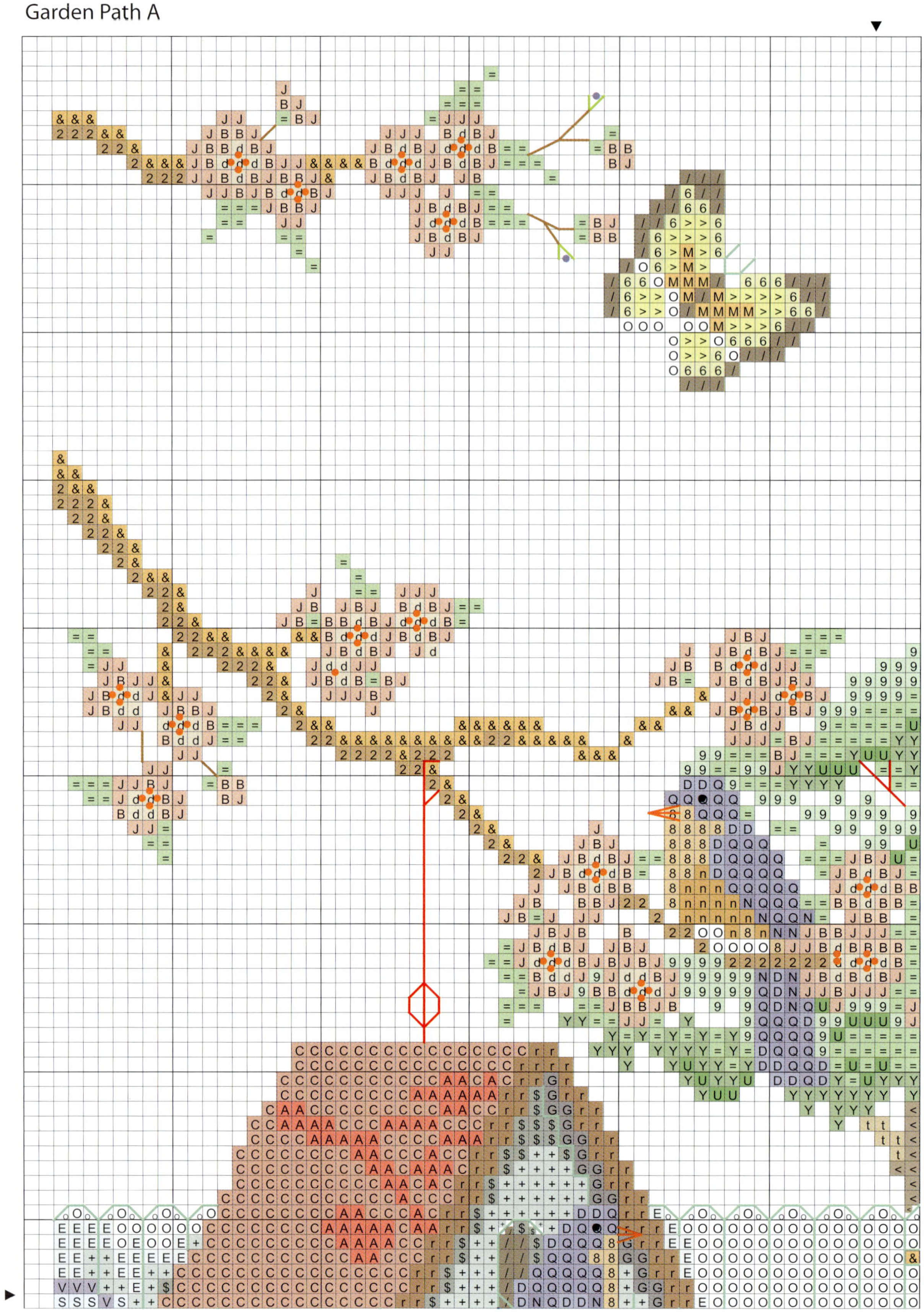

Note: Color key can be found on page 2.

Garden Path B

Gray area indicates last row of previous section of design.

Garden Path C

Note: Color key can be found on page 2.

Garden Path D

Gray area indicates last row of previous section of design.

Spring Birds

Designed by Barbara Sestok

Bring the outdoors in with this set of pretty bird coasters. They will brighten up any surface in your home and delight all who see them.

Note: Please read all instructions on page 24 before beginning.

Stitch Count (each design) = 42w × 42h

FABRIC SIZE (EACH DESIGN)

- One 10" × 10" (25.4cm × 25.4cm) piece of 14-ct. white aida

DESIGN SIZE (EACH DESIGN)

- 14-ct. = 3" × 3" (7.6cm × 7.6cm)

FINISHING MATERIALS

- Four 4¼" wood coasters with 3" design openings

INSTRUCTIONS

Center the design and begin stitching. Work cross stitches and quarter stitches with two strands of cotton embroidery floss. Use one strand of cotton embroidery floss to work backstitches and French knots. Use a pressing cloth to carefully iron the needlework from the back before inserting into the coasters according to the manufacturer's instructions.

CROSS STITCH

ANCHOR		DMC	COLOR
403	X	310	Black
399	R	318	Light Steel Gray
1025	A	347	Very Dark Salmon
011	C	350	Medium Coral
009	B	352	Light Coral
401	S	413	Dark Pewter Gray
238	H	703	Chartreuse
295	J	726	Light Topaz
131	E	798	Dark Delft Blue
130	D	809	Delft Blue
379	N	840	Medium Beige Brown
378	M	841	Light Beige Brown
397	Q	3024	Very Light Brown Gray
267	G	3346	Hunter Green
1050	P	3781	Dark Mocha Brown
306	I	3820	Dark Straw
365	L	3826	Golden Brown
1003	K	3853	Dark Autumn Gold
002	O	3865	Winter White

FRENCH KNOT

ANCHOR		DMC	COLOR
002	•	3865	Winter White

BACKSTITCH

ANCHOR	DMC	COLOR
403	310	Black
399	318	Light Steel Gray
238	703	Chartreuse
295	726	Light Topaz
1050	3781	Dark Mocha Brown
1003	3853	Dark Autumn Gold
002	3865	Winter White

CROSS STITCH

ANCHOR		DMC	COLOR
403	X	310	Black
399	R	318	Light Steel Gray
1025	A	347	Very Dark Salmon
011	C	350	Medium Coral
009	B	352	Light Coral
401	S	413	Dark Pewter Gray
238	H	703	Chartreuse
295	J	726	Light Topaz
131	E	798	Dark Delft Blue
130	D	809	Delft Blue
379	N	840	Medium Beige Brown
378	M	841	Light Beige Brown
397	Q	3024	Very Light Brown Gray
267	G	3346	Hunter Green
1050	P	3781	Dark Mocha Brown
306	I	3820	Dark Straw
365	L	3826	Golden Brown
1003	K	3853	Dark Autumn Gold
002	O	3865	Winter White

FRENCH KNOT

ANCHOR		DMC	COLOR
002	•	3865	Winter White

BACKSTITCH

ANCHOR		DMC	COLOR
403	—	310	Black
399	—	318	Light Steel Gray
238	—	703	Chartreuse
295	—	726	Light Topaz
1050	—	3781	Dark Mocha Brown
1003	—	3853	Dark Autumn Gold
002	—	3865	Winter White

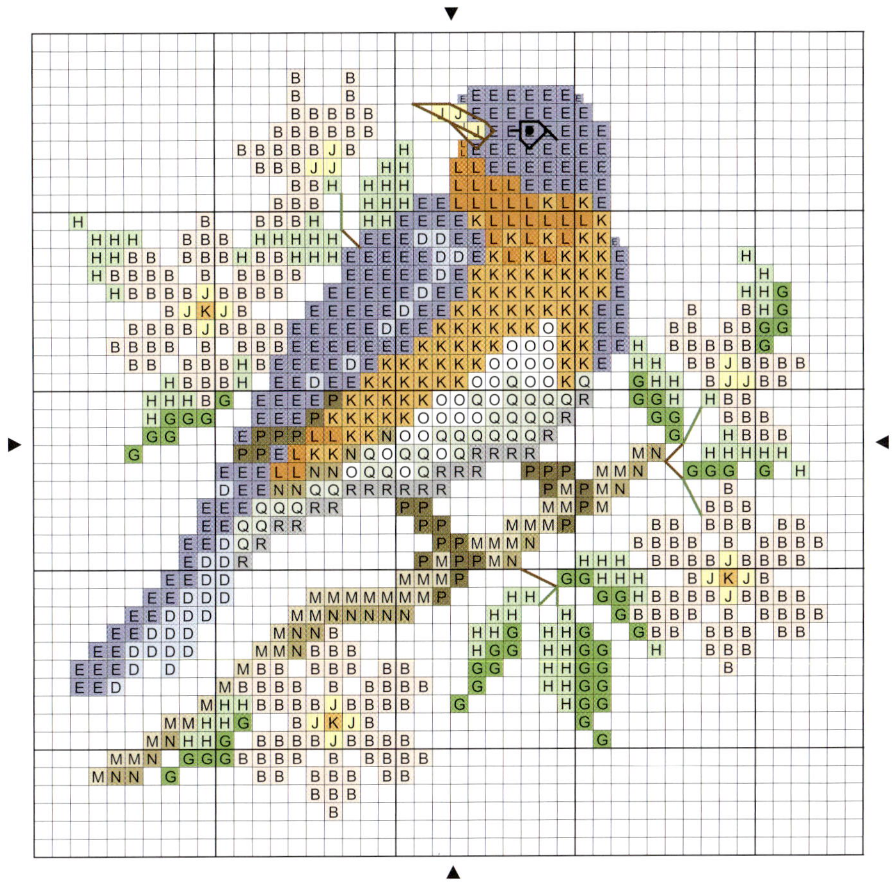

Project Tip

Prevent Twisting

During the movement of stitching, the needle naturally twists, which can cause loops and knots in the thread. To prevent this, work several stitches, then make note of which way the thread unwinds when you hang it straight down from your work. Give your needle a partial turn in that direction with each stitch to keep the thread from twisting.

Elegant Cranes

Designed by Linda Bird

A garland of lotus flowers on a backdrop of rich black fabric creates an elegant frame for these cranes in flight.

Note: Please read all instructions on page 24 before beginning.

Stitch Count = 181w × 125h

FABRIC SIZE

- One 17" × 21" (43.2cm × 53.3cm) piece of 14-ct. Black Damask Aida by Zweigart®

DESIGN SIZE

- 14-ct. = 12⁷/₈" × 8⁷/₈" (32.7cm × 22.5cm)

FINISHING MATERIALS

- One yard of pink coordinating fabric for back and bias strips
- 1¼ yards of ¼"-wide cording
- Matching sewing thread
- Polyester fiberfill
- Coordinating tassels

GENERAL INSTRUCTIONS

Center the design and begin stitching. Work cross stitches, quarter stitches, backstitches, and French knots with two strands of cotton embroidery floss. Use a couching stitch for the cranes' necks with six strands of DMC® 3033/Anchor 391 for the laid thread and one strand to couch. Use a pressing cloth to carefully iron the needlework from the back before finishing.

FINISHING INSTRUCTIONS

Use a ½" seam allowance for all sewing unless otherwise specified. Center and trim the needlework to within 1" of the stitching. Use the needlework to cut a backing piece from the coordinating pink fabric. Cut 1½"-wide bias strips of coordinating pink fabric and piece together to form one 45"-long strip. Fold in half lengthwise with wrong sides together. Insert cording into the fold and sew tightly along the edge of the cording using a zipper foot. Making sure the cording is flush with the edge of the stitching, start at the top left of the needlework and sew the piping around the pillow, keeping the seam close to the cording.

With right sides together, sew the pillow front to the back, sewing tight to the cording and leaving an opening for turning. Trim the side and bottom seam allowances to ¼". Turn the pillow right side out and iron using a pressing cloth. Stuff the pillow firmly with polyester fiberfill and slip stitch the opening closed. Tack tassels to each corner of the pillow.

CROSS STITCH

ANCHOR		DMC	COLOR
001	•	White	White
387	A	Ecru	Ecru
897	L	221	Very Dark Shell Pink
895	H	223	Light Shell Pink
893	E	224	Very Light Pink
1026	D	225	Ultra Very Light Shell Pink
400	V	317	Pewter Gray
398	X	415	Pearl Gray
860	B	522	Fern Green
859	I	523	Light Fern Green
858	G	524	Very Light Fern Green
392	S	642	Dark Beige Gray
845	J	730	Very Dark Olive Green
861	U	935	Dark Avocado Green
269	Z	936	Very Dark Avocado Green
844	T	3012	Medium Khaki Green
842	P	3013	Light Khaki Green
391	R	3033	Very Light Mocha Brown
896	F	3721	Dark Shell Pink
393	K	3790	Ultra Dark Beige Gray

FRENCH KNOT

ANCHOR		DMC	COLOR
403	•	310	Black
391	•	3033	Very Light Mocha Brown

BACKSTITCH

ANCHOR		DMC	COLOR
403	—	310	Black

COUCHING STITCH

ANCHOR		DMC	COLOR
391	—	3033	Very Light Mocha Brown

ELEGANT CRANES CHART DIAGRAM

B	D
A	C

Elegant Cranes A

Gray area indicates last row of previous section of design.

Elegant Cranes B

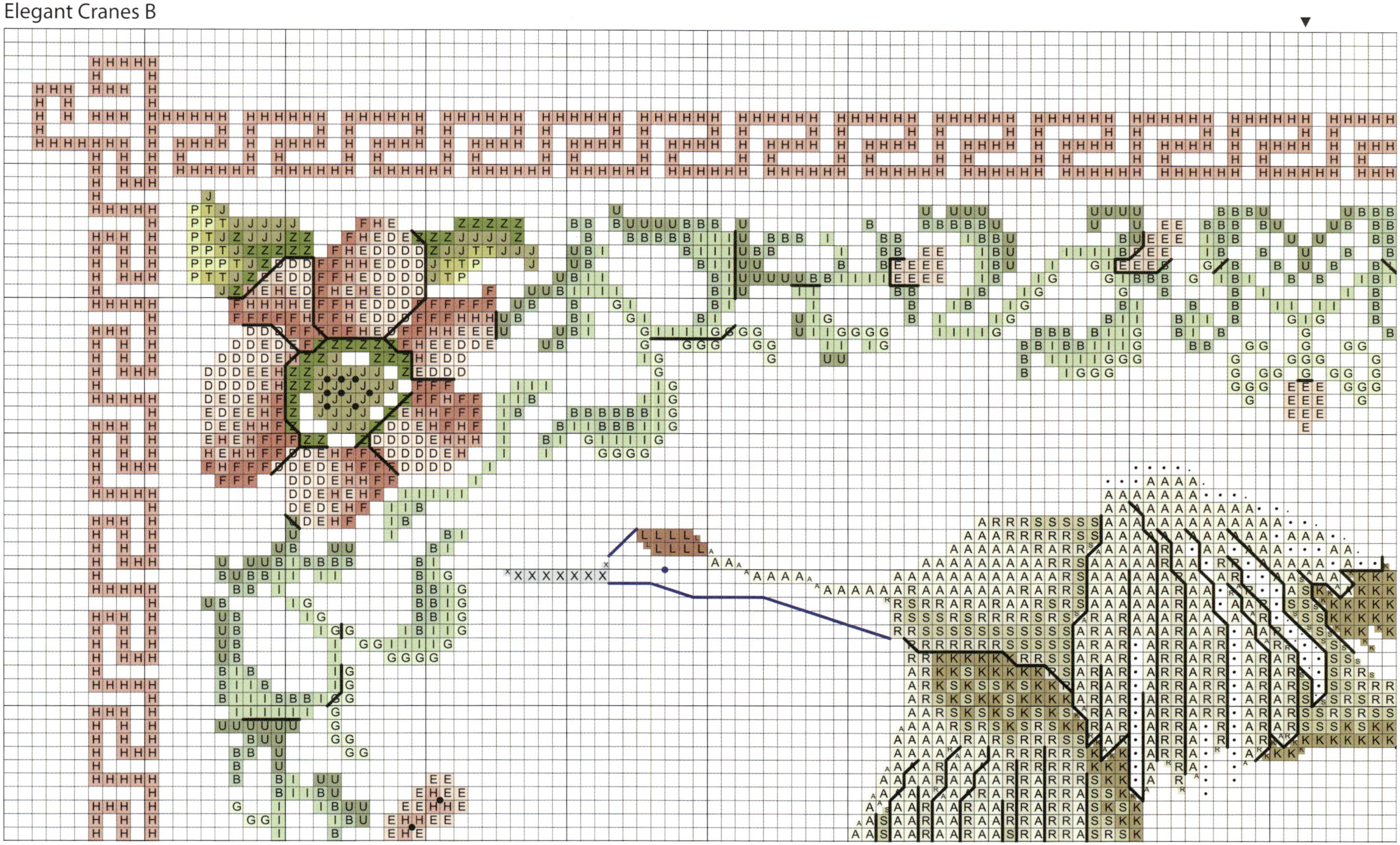

Note: Color key can be found on page 12.

Elegant Cranes C

Gray area indicates last row of previous section of design.

Elegant Cranes D

Note: Color key can be found on page 12.

In Everything, Give Thanks!

Designed by Gail Bussi

Giving thanks is not just reserved for the fourth Thursday in November. Express your thankfulness every day with this joyous piece.

Note: Please read all instructions on page 24 before beginning.

Stitch Count = 140w × 105h

FABRIC SIZE

- One 18" × 16" (45.7cm × 40.6cm) piece of 28-ct. Antique White Jobelan® by Wichelt Imports (stitched over two threads)

DESIGN SIZE

- 28-ct. = 10" × 7½" (25.4cm × 19.1cm)

FINISHING MATERIALS

- ½ yard of coordinating fabric for backing and binding
- One 13½" × 11" piece of lightweight cotton batting
- One 13½" × 11" piece of stiff interfacing
- Basting spray (optional)
- Matching sewing thread

GENERAL INSTRUCTIONS

Center the design and begin stitching over two fabric threads. Work cross stitches, half cross stitches, and quarter stitches with two strands of cotton embroidery floss. Use two strands of cotton embroidery floss to work the lettering and one strand of floss for all other backstitches. Work French knots with one strand of cotton embroidery floss. Use a pressing cloth to carefully iron the needlework from the back before finishing.

FINISHING INSTRUCTIONS

Make sure the design is centered and trim the needlework to 13½" × 11" (there should be a 1¾" border around the stitched design). Cut a piece of backing fabric the same size. Place the back panel wrong side up on a work surface. Place a piece of cotton batting, then a piece of stiff interfacing, and then the needlework right side up on top of the back panel. Baste around the perimeter ¼" from the edge.

Cut 2½" strips of the coordinating fabric and piece together to form a strip at least 50" long. Fold in half along the length with wrong sides together and press to create a binding. With the cut edges aligned and using a ⅜" seam allowance, sew the binding around the needlework side of the piece, folding to form a miter at each corner. Fold and press the binding to the back and hand-stitch in place.

If desired, create a hanging loop by cutting a 2" × 13" strip from leftover fabric. Fold in half along the length with right sides together and press. Sew along the cut edge using a ¼" seam allowance, turn right sides out, and press. Attach ends to the top back of the wall hanging with a few hand stitches.

GIVE THANKS CHART DIAGRAM

B	D
A	C

In everything give thanks
Sing a happy song

Give Thanks A

CROSS STITCH

ANCHOR		DMC	COLOR
240	7	164	Light Forest Green
400	G	317	Pewter Gray
215	3	320	Medium Pistachio Green
235	9	414	Dark Steel Gray
374	6	420	Dark Hazelnut Brown
943	W	422	Light Hazelnut Brown
858	L	524	Very Light Fern Green
830	B	644	Medium Beige Gray
301	N	744	Pale Yellow
1012	8	754	Light Peach
390	H	822	Light Beige Gray
1034	O	931	Medium Antique Blue
1033	A	932	Light Antique Blue

CROSS STITCH

ANCHOR		DMC	COLOR
073	E	963	Ultra Very Light Dusty Rose
393	Y	3022	Medium Brown Gray
1040	P	3023	Light Brown Gray
903	Z	3032	Medium Mocha Brown
391	e	3033	Very Light Mocha Brown
888	h	3045	Dark Yellow Beige
887	F	3046	Medium Yellow Beige
852	R	3047	Light Yellow Beige
266	J	3347	Medium Yellow Green
264	4	3348	Light Yellow Green
074	5	3354	Light Dusty Rose
260	U	3364	Pine Green
076	T	3731	Very Dark Dusty Rose

CROSS STITCH

ANCHOR		DMC	COLOR
075	1	3733	Dusty Rose
1031	V	3753	Ultra Very Light Antique Blue
778	a	3774	Very Light Desert Sand
393	S	3790	Ultra Dark Beige Gray
386	K	3823	Ultra Pale Yellow
090	M	3836	Light Grape
002	2	3865	Winter White

FRENCH KNOT

ANCHOR		DMC	COLOR
273	•	3787	Dark Brown Gray
002	•	3865	Winter White

BACKSTITCH

ANCHOR		DMC	COLOR
1034	—	931	Medium Antique Blue
262	—	3363	Medium Pine Green
273	—	3787	Dark Brown Gray
002	—	3865	Winter White

Give Thanks B

Gray area indicates last row of previous section of design.

Give Thanks C

CROSS STITCH

ANCHOR		DMC	COLOR
240	7	164	Light Forest Green
400	G	317	Pewter Gray
215	3	320	Medium Pistachio Green
235	9	414	Dark Steel Gray
374	6	420	Dark Hazelnut Brown
943	W	422	Light Hazelnut Brown
858	L	524	Very Light Fern Green
830	B	644	Medium Beige Gray
301	N	744	Pale Yellow
1012	8	754	Light Peach
390	H	822	Light Beige Gray
1034	O	931	Medium Antique Blue
1033	A	932	Light Antique Blue

CROSS STITCH

ANCHOR		DMC	COLOR
073	E	963	Ultra Very Light Dusty Rose
393	Y	3022	Medium Brown Gray
1040	P	3023	Light Brown Gray
903	Z	3032	Medium Mocha Brown
391	e	3033	Very Light Mocha Brown
888	h	3045	Dark Yellow Beige
887	F	3046	Medium Yellow Beige
852	R	3047	Light Yellow Beige
266	J	3347	Medium Yellow Green
264	4	3348	Light Yellow Green
074	5	3354	Light Dusty Rose
260	U	3364	Pine Green
076	T	3731	Very Dark Dusty Rose

CROSS STITCH

ANCHOR		DMC	COLOR
075	1	3733	Dusty Rose
1031	V	3753	Ultra Very Light Antique Blue
778	a	3774	Very Light Desert Sand
393	S	3790	Ultra Dark Beige Gray
386	K	3823	Ultra Pale Yellow
090	M	3836	Light Grape
002	2	3865	Winter White

FRENCH KNOT

ANCHOR		DMC	COLOR
273	• (black)	3787	Dark Brown Gray
002	• (light blue)	3865	Winter White

BACKSTITCH

ANCHOR		DMC	COLOR
1034	— (red)	931	Medium Antique Blue
262	— (dark blue)	3363	Medium Pine Green
273	— (black)	3787	Dark Brown Gray
002	— (green)	3865	Winter White

Gray area indicates last row of previous section of design.

Give Thanks D

General Instructions

Getting Started

For most projects, the starting point is at the center. Every chart has arrows that indicate the horizontal and vertical centers. With your finger, trace along the grid to the point where the two centers meet. Compare a symbol at the center of the chart to the key and choose which floss color to stitch first. To find the center of the fabric, fold it into quarters and finger-crease.

Cut the floss into 15" lengths and separate all six strands. Recombine the appropriate number of strands and thread them into a blunt-tip needle. Unless otherwise indicated, use two strands of floss to work cross stitches, half cross stitches, and quarter cross stitches. Use one strand of floss to work backstitches, straight stitches, French knots, and lazy daisy stitches.

To Secure Thread at the Beginning

The most common way to secure the beginning tail of the thread is to hold it on the wrong side of the fabric under the first four or five stitches.

To Secure Thread at the End

To finish, slip the threaded needle under previously stitched threads on the wrong side of the fabric for four or five stitches, weaving the thread back and forth a few times. Clip the thread.

Cross Stitch

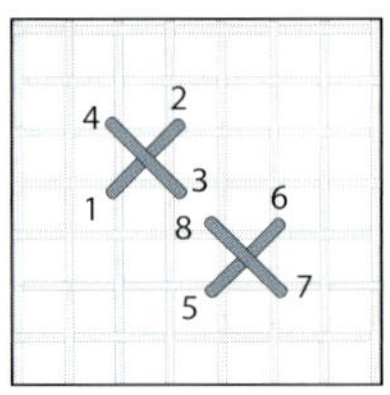

Make one cross stitch for each symbol on the chart. For horizontal rows, stitch the first diagonal of each stitch in the row. Work back across the row, completing each stitch. On linen and evenweave fabrics, work the stitches over two threads as shown in the diagram. For aida cloth, each stitch fills one square. You also can work cross stitches in the reverse direction. Remember to embroider the stitches uniformly—that is, always work the top half of each stitch in the same direction.

Half Cross Stitches

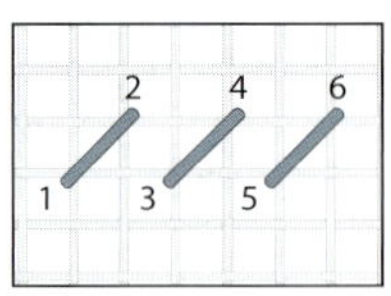

A half cross stitch is a single diagonal or half a cross stitch. They are indicated on the chart by a diagonal colored symbol.

Quarter Cross Stitches

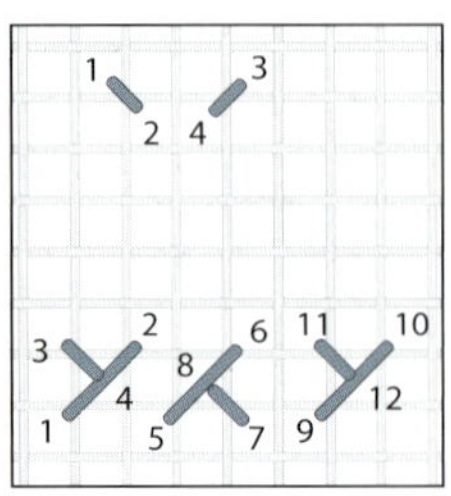

To obtain rounded shapes in a design, use quarter and three-quarter cross stitches. On linen and evenweave fabrics, a quarter stitch will extend from the corner to the center intersection of the threads. To make quarter cross stitches on aida cloth, estimate the center of the square. Three-quarter cross stitches combine a quarter cross stitch with a half cross stitch. Both stitches may slant in any direction.

Backstitches

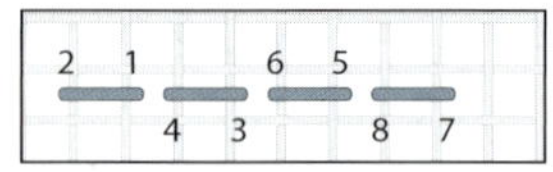

Working from right to left, bring the needle up from the back side of the fabric, one stitch length from your starting point. Begin the next stitch by inserting the needle at your starting point and back up two stitch lengths away. Continue, keeping all the stitches the same length.

Straight Stitches

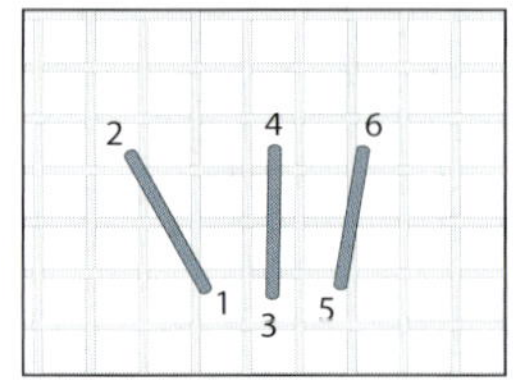

Bring the needle up from the back side of the fabric, then bring the needle down through the fabric in the desired spot to make a stitch of the desired length.

French Knot

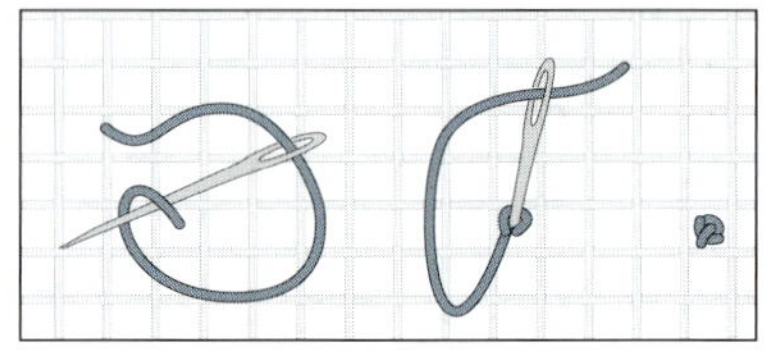

Bring the threaded needle through the fabric and wrap the floss around the needle as shown. Tighten the twists and return the needle through the fabric in the same place. The floss will slide through the wrapped thread to make the knot.

Lazy Daisy

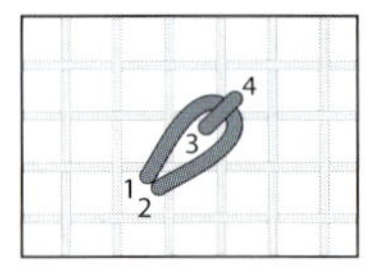

Bring the needle to the front of the fabric and return to the back through the same hole, forming a loop. Slide the tip of the needle under two or more threads, then bring it to the front of the fabric. Slip the loop under the needle tip. Pull gently until the loop lies smoothly on the fabric. Push the needle to the back, forming a tack stitch over the end of the loop.

Couching

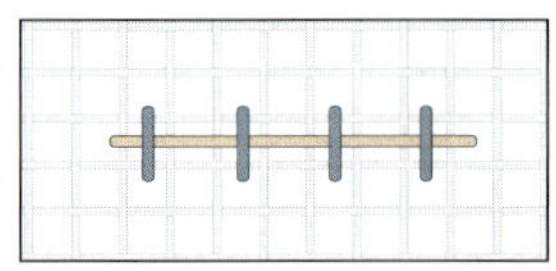

Use two needles to work a line of couching. Bring the thicker couched thread through the fabric at the beginning of the line designated on the chart and to the back at the end. Roughly align it in the position indicated on the chart. Bring the thinner couching thread through the fabric four threads (unless otherwise specified on the chart) beyond the entry point of the couched thread, over it, and to the back in the next hole. Move four threads along the line of the couched thread and repeat the couching. Continue along the entire length of the couched thread.

Produced by Herrschners, Inc., for distribution exclusively by Leisure Arts, Inc., 104 Champs Blvd., STE 100, Maumelle, AR 72113-6738, leisurearts.com.

Copyright © 2016 by Herrschners, Inc. All rights reserved. This publication is protected under federal copyright laws. Reproduction of this publication or any other Leisure Arts publication, including publications which are out of print, is prohibited unless specifically authorized. This includes, but is not limited to, any form of reproduction or distribution on or through the Internet, including posting, scanning, or e-mail transmission.

We have made every effort to ensure that these instructions are accurate and complete. We cannot, however, be responsible for human error, typographical mistakes, or variations in individual work.